The History of
SCOTLAND

Text by Chris Ta...

Colin Baxter Photography Ltd, Grantown-on-Spey, Scotland

Contents

Dunnottar Castle: *(opposite) The spectacular promontory thrusting into the chilly North Sea from the Kincardineshire coast has served as Iron-Age fort, Pictish dun, medieval castle and state prison. Legend tells that the stronghold once housed a magic shining shield guarded by a ferocious old hag. In reality, Dunnottar was where the Honours of Scotland, the nation's crown jewels, were hidden from Oliver Cromwell's 'Roundheads' in 1651-2.*

The History of Scotland

Mention Scotland, and most people think of whisky, tartan and bagpipes. Ask them to name three famous Scots, and the chances are they will come up with Mary, Queen of Scots, William Wallace and 'Bonnie Prince Charlie'. Quiz them about famous historic events and the smart money will be on the Battle of Bannockburn, the Massacre of Glencoe and the Highland Clearances. All are perfectly valid responses. But Scotland's history is far richer, and its contribution to the world far more immense, than these familiar icons might suggest.

To whisky, tartan and bagpipes add penicillin and painkillers, pedal bicycles, pneumatic tyres and ships' propellers, telephones, televisions, radar and the rest. To Mary, 'Braveheart' and 'B.P.C.' add David Hume, the greatest philosopher of his age, James Hutton, the father of modern geology, Robert Burns, the national bard, and countless others. And though fighting the English and feuding amongst themselves came second nature to Scots, they also found time to drive the industrial revolution, build railroads across the Rockies, delve deep into Africa, and create the economic miracle that is Hong Kong. For a wee country on the edge of Europe, Scotland has consistently 'punched above its weight'.

Scots have been around for over 10,000 years. During that time they have been invaded by Romans, Angles and Vikings. The Romans came and went,

Glamis Castle, Angus: James Francis Edward Stuart, the 'Old Pretender', who stayed here in January 1716, declared there was no finer edifice than the residence of the Earls of Stathmore. It was the childhood home of the late Queen Elizabeth the Queen Mother.

Mary, Queen of Scots:
Scotland's famous
sovereign lived for
44 years. 12 years
were spent in France,
18 in England – and
just 14 in Scotland.

Prince Charles
Edward Stuart:
(opposite) The
would-be king of
Great Britain spent
just one year on
Scottish soil, during
the '45 Jacobite
Rising.

St Columba. When, around 843, their king, Kenneth son of Alpin (Cenáid mac Ailpín), became king of the Picts, Scotland's oldest indigenous people, the nation we call Scotland was created.

It was another union centuries later that brought an end to the most hostile 'take-over bid' of them all. In 1603, within the hallowed walls of Westminster Abbey, King James VI of Scotland was crowned King James I of England. At one stroke, five centuries of bloodshed were brought to an end. Countless heroes had died in the cause – foremost amongst them 'Braveheart' himself. Today, when the Scottish Saltire and English Rose come crunching together, they do so on the sports field not the battlefield.

Since the creation of the United Kingdom, Scotland has more than held its own. A galaxy of famous scientists, inventors, industrialists, philosophers, fighters, writers and politicians have left a lasting memorial not only in the land of their birth but across the globe. Thirteen out of 53 British prime ministers have had Scots blood coursing through their veins, as have 11 American presidents. One Scot founded the Bank of England, another the American navy, and a third turned an Australian penal colony into a proud country. That man was Lachlan Macquarrie, a confirmed 'teetotaller. Now he wouldn't have put whisky at the top of his list!

leaving behind little but a defensive wall that was their Empire's most northerly frontier. The Angles too came and went, leaving behind something much more long-lasting, the English language. And a visit to the Northern Isles of Orkney and Shetland is sufficient to show that the Vikings are still very much with us, at least in spirit. Even the Gaels themselves were invaders, crossing from Ireland in the centuries after Christ's birth, bringing the Gaelic tongue with them, as well as the Christian gospel, courtesy of

Ancient Scotland

Glen Affric,
Inverness-shire:
The shores around
Loch Affric are still
dotted about with
remnants of the
ancient Caledonian
pine forest that
sprang up after the
last Ice Age ended
11,000 years ago. It
grew to cover vast
areas of Scotland,
though now only
about one percent
remains in scattered
isolated locations.

SCOTLAND BC

Mankind first set foot in Scotland 11,000 years ago. What name they gave to the densely forested land they encountered, where reindeer grazed and polecat prowled, is a mystery, like so much of their story. They were a restless people, forever on the search for food, remaining in one place only long enough to leave behind the odd campfire.

For 3000 years, these Mesolithic hunter-gatherers roamed the land. Slowly they put down roots. The wild landscape became home to them, as they returned year on year to familiar haunts. Their primitive stone tools, capable only of catching fish and game, developed into implements able to tame the environment and till the soil. By 4000 BC our Neolithic ancestors had become Scotland's first farmers.

The more settled communities began to build more permanently. Remains of their houses and fields, ceremonial places and burial tombs are scattered across Scotland, but it is in the heart of Neolithic Orkney, amid the beguiling ruins of Skara Brae, built more than 5000 years ago, before Stonehenge was conceived, and abandoned as the great pyramid at Cheops was nearing

Jarlshof, Shetland: Around 100 years ago, violent storms ripped open the low cliffs near Sumburgh to reveal an extraordinary settlement site stretching from Neolithic times, more than 4,000 years ago, all the way up to the 17th century AD.

Calanais Standing Stones, Isle of Lewis: Quite why our Neolithic ancestors chose to build this impressive stone circle around 5,000 years ago is a mystery, but it possibly served as some kind of astronomical observatory.

completion, that we perhaps get closest to their world, so different from our own – and yet with an eerily familiar feel, particularly those cosy homes, with their beds and dressing-tables.

More difficult to comprehend are their great ceremonial circles and monumental tombs. What they did inside the Ring of Brodgar, or who they buried within Maes Howe, are more of those eternal mysteries, but their very construction is powerful proof of an intelligent people with a strong sense of community.

The climate in those far-off times was comfortably warm, sufficient for wheat

to flourish in Shetland. But a decline set in around 1000 BC, and so, apparently, did man's ability to live in peace with their neighbour. The skill of working copper metal, introduced from Europe

Dun Carloway Broch, Isle of Lewis: *Brochs are a fortification unique to Scotland. Excavations at this well-preserved example revealed that people had been living inside it, on and off, throughout much of the first millennium AD.*

ROMANS, PICTS & BRITONS

In AD 79, General Agricola, under orders from the Roman emperor Vespasian, entered North Britain with his legions and reached the River Tay. Four years later, at the battle of Mons Graupius (an eighteenth-century clerical error gave us the name Grampian), they defeated a confederation of tribes called the Caledonians (Dunkeld means 'fortress of the Caledones'). Leading the Caledonian warriors was Calgacus, 'the swordsman'; he is the first 'Scot' named in our annals.

about 2000 BC, came to be used not just to create better tools and more attractive jewellery but to produce weapons. Perhaps the cooler, wetter weather, which encouraged the growth of peat and reduced the amount of cultivable land, placed undue pressure on communities, leading to greater conflict.

With the coming of the Romans, Scotland stepped into history. We learn from them the names of rivers, of mountains and settlements.

The first truly defensive structures – hillforts – appeared around 2500 years ago, about the same time that iron-working technology arrived. Some hillforts were sprawling tribal centres, others were home to just a few families. As the prehistoric world drew to a close, lofty stone towers (brochs) appeared. When the Christian era dawned, the tribes sheltering behind these defences faced a new threat.

Crannog, Loch Tay: *Crannogs, or loch-dwellings, were once common throughout Scotland. There are eighteen in Loch Tay alone. One has recently been excavated, leading to the construction of this authentic replica of the 2,500-year-old house.*

We learn also that 16 tribes inhabited Scotland. Those in the north remained implacably opposed to Rome throughout the three centuries of attempted conquest; from them would emerge the tribal confederation the Romans referred to as Picts or 'painted people'.

The southern tribes, on the other hand, came more fully under the Roman yoke, tolerating the invader. They included the Damnonii, from the Firth of Clyde and the Votadini of Lothian. Yet these tribes too re-emerged after the fall of the Roman Empire with new identities – the Damnonii as the Britons of Strathclyde, with their 'capital city' at Dumbarton Rock, and the Votadini as the Gododdin, centred on Edinburgh's Castle Rock.

Ring of Brodgar, Mainland, Orkney: Sixty tall stones originally formed the 'ring' of this 5,000-year-old ceremonial complex.

The Romans

Did you know... Imperial Rome built its most northerly frontier in Scotland? Fine stretches of the Antonine Wall, built for the Emperor Antinus Pius in 142, can still be seen striding across Scotland's Central Belt between Glasgow and Edinburgh.

Dark Age Scotland

COMING OF THE GAELS

By 400, the invader had become the invaded as Picts and Britons repeatedly attacked beyond Hadrian's Wall. By now, though, new threats were emerging from the west.

Fighting alongside the Picts and Britons in those final years of Roman rule was a people the Romans called *Scoti*, but who called themselves Gaels. Tradition holds that the Gaels, under Fergus Mór 'the Great', crossed from Northern Ireland about 500 and settled in Argyll, but it now seems more likely that their migration to the land that now bears their name began much earlier. By 600, their kingdom of Dalriada extended from Kintyre to Ardnamurchan. They brought with them a new language, Gaelic; Argyll, *Earra Ghaidheal*, means 'coastland of the Gael'.

They also brought with them a new religion, Christianity, chiefly through the person of Columba. From his island monastery on Iona, founded around 563, Columba made several missions into Pictland spreading the Christian gospel. During one such mission, to the court of King Bridei beside the River Ness, he saved a companion from the jaws of a fierce water-beast (*aquatilis bestia*), our first recorded sighting of the monster we know better as 'Nessie'.

Columba was not the first to bring Christianity to Scotland, however. Around a century earlier, St Ninian had established his

Iona Abbey, Argyll:
The lovingly restored medieval abbey on the tiny island of Iona stands over the very site where St Columba founded his monastery around 563 and where he was buried in 597.

missionary base at Whithorn, and in the museum there visitors can see the 'Latinus Stone', Scotland's oldest Christian memorial.

ANGLES AND VIKINGS

Columba died on Iona in 597. Already a new aggressor was emerging from the south to threaten the Picts, Britons and Gaels. The Angles, a pagan Germanic race, were by now firmly established in the north-east of the land that is now named after them – England.

Around 600, Mynyddog 'the Mighty', king of the Gododdin, set out with his war-band from the rocky fortress of Din Eidyn to confront them. He was humiliatingly defeated. The Angles seized the initiative and invaded Mynyddog's kingdom. In 638, they captured Din Eidyn, and renamed it Edinburgh. The Gododdin were history.

The Angles did not stop there. They pushed northward into Pictland. But they overreached themselves and in 685 King Ecgfrith of Northumbria and most of his army were slaughtered by

Lewis Chessmen:
These wonderful walrus ivory chess-pieces, made somewhere in the Viking world around 1100, were found quite by chance in 1831 in sand dunes close to Uig, on the west side of Lewis.

Dunadd Fort, Argyll:
This rocky fortress was a royal residence of the Gaelic kings of Dalriada in the 6th century. On its summit, carved into the rock, are a basin, an image of a boar, and two human footprints, probably used during the inauguration of a new king.

the Picts at Nechtansmere, in Angus. The wonderful Pictish stone in the churchyard at Aberlemno, near the battle site, depicts a battle scene, most likely King Bridei's victory over Ecgrith.

The Angles had no option but to retrench south of the Forth.

The Anglian menace encouraged closer dialogue between the threatened Picts, Britons and Gaels. It is a confusing web of inter-relationships between the various royal dynasties; King Bridei himself was a Strathclyde Briton and not a Pict. The matter was only finally resolved around 843 when Kenneth mac Alpin, 'son of Alpin' and king of the Scots, became king of the Picts also. The history of Pictland was over. Scotland was born.

Kenneth I died in 858 not in his native Argyll but in the Earn valley near Perth. The Scots' move eastward was no simple act of conquest; it had been forced on them by an

Moot Hill, Scone:
This ancient Pictish king-making site continued in use after Kenneth I united the Picts and Scots around 843. In 1296 Edward I of England removed the famous Stone of Scone, or 'Stone of Destiny', to London; the one in the foreground is a replica.

aggressor altogether more ruthless even than the Angles.

In 795, Viking pirates from Norway (called Norsemen) descended on Iona and ransacked Columba's monastery; further raids quickly followed. Soon the children of these summer raiders were settling around the northern and western coasts of Scotland, forcing the Scots to move their power-centres eastward. Royal seats at Dunadd and elsewhere were abandoned; so too was Iona for a time. The famous Book of Kells was taken to Ireland, but some of Columba's relics were removed to Dunkeld, chosen as the new headquarters of the Scottish Church. The Moot Hill ('meeting hill') at Scone, near Perth, became the new king-making place. Down the centuries a glittering array of sovereigns have journeyed to Scone to receive the acclamation of their subjects, including Macbeth (1040), John Balliol (1292), Robert 'the Bruce' (1306) and Charles II, the last, on 1 January 1651.

The Senchus Census

Did you know... Britain's earliest census was not William the Conqueror's Domesday Book of the 1080s, but the *Senchus Fer nAlban*, carried out for a king of Scots 400 years earlier? The *Senchus* records in extraordinary detail the composition of each of the four kindreds, or clans. Apparently, the king could call on a fighting force of 2000 men in 140 ships.

Edinburgh Castle:
In the Dark Ages, the castle rock was known as Din Eidyn. The present castle, founded in the early 1100s, was one of the first in Scotland.

Medieval and Renaissance Scotland

THE NORMANS

In 1018, Malcolm II defeated the Anglo-Saxons at Carham, effectively fixing Scotland's border on the River Tweed. When he died in 1034, his grandson, Duncan I succeeded. This was the Duncan whom Macbeth killed in 1040 to become king himself. Duncan's son, Malcolm III, took revenge in 1057.

The Celtic blood coursed through Malcolm III's veins, but the moment he set eyes on the saintly Saxon princess, Margaret, he was besotted. They married at Dunfermline about 1070 and she bore him eight children. The youngest boy, David I, brought Scotland out from its Celtic shadow into the full light of continental medieval Europe.

As a boy, David travelled south to the Norman-English court for his sister's wedding to William the Conqueror's son, Henry I. There he observed the Anglo-Normans' feudal ways, and when he returned to Scotland, in 1113, he was thoroughly Normanised. The changes he initiated, continued by his grandsons, Malcolm IV and William 'the Lion', transformed the country. Few aspects of life escaped change.

There wasn't a Norman conquest of Scotland as such, but there was a tidal wave of Anglo-Norman immigration throughout the 12th century. The legacy of these immigrants lives on in many

Jedburgh Abbey, Scottish Borders: (opposite) In the 12th century, Scotland was transformed from a Celtic kingdom to a feudal state. No aspect of national life was left unaffected. This included the national church. The diocesan structure was overhauled, and parishes introduced. Among the many monasteries built was the splendid Augustinian abbey of Jedburgh, a wonderful feast of Romanesque and Gothic architecture.

Melrose Abbey Scottish Borders: The Cistercian monks of Melrose were renowned sheep farmers. At one stage they had some 15,000 sheep grazing on the Southern Uplands.

John Balliol at Edward I of England's Feet: The English king presided over King John's enthronement at Scone in 1292, and also his abdication at Montrose four years later. Balliol's downfall in 1296 was the prelude to the bloody Wars of Independence.

of the end of Norse dominion in the west. By 1200, Walter's son, Alan, had reclaimed Bute, and in 1263 at Largs, on the Ayrshire coast, Hakon IV's attempt to reassert his sovereignty came to grief. Three years later, King Magnus Hakonson and Alexander III of Scotland set their seals to the Treaty of Perth, which brought the Hebrides back under Scottish rule after four centuries.

THE WARS OF INDEPENDENCE

Alexander III tragically died in 1286; so too did his heir, Margaret 'Maid of Norway', in 1290. Scotland was thrown into turmoil. Edward I of England seized his chance and in March 1296 crossed the Tweed and butchered most of the population of Berwick, then Scotland's chief town. Edward 'Longshanks' was beginning to earn his other nickname 'Hammer of the Scots'.

Scottish surnames – for example, Bruce (from Brus (now Brix), in Normandy) and, most famous of all, Stewart, the ancestors of the British royal house, who had once served as stewards of the bishops of Dol, in Brittany.

It was Walter, the high stewart of Scotland, who in 1164 killed Somerled, the last of the powerful Celtic-Norse leaders, in battle near Renfrew. Somerled's death marked the beginning

Edward's chances of conquering Scotland certainly looked promising. His army, battle-hardened from campaigns in France and Wales, faced Scotland's common army of townsmen and country folk. Without a king, they found a leader in William Wallace, son of a minor laird. Within the year Wallace won a remarkable victory at Stirling Bridge (September 1297). The outcome brought fresh hope to a nation staring into the abyss.

Wallace's success, though, was short-lived. He tasted defeat at Falkirk in

Norwegian Influences

Did you know... most of north and west Scotland was Norwegian for centuries? Dingwall, 11 miles (17km) from Inverness, comes from the Norse *thing vollr*, 'field of the court of justice', and as late as 1200 Arran and Bute were still part of Norway.

the following year, and after a determined rearguard action he was betrayed and captured near Glasgow in 1305. A humiliating and cruel torture at the hands of Edward I followed, in which he was dragged through the streets of London, hanged, cut down while still alive and disembowelled. No sooner had the last breath left his body than the 'Braveheart' legend was born.

A great nobleman assumed Wallace's mantle – Robert 'the Bruce', earl of Carrick, whose grandfather, also Robert, had contended with John Balliol, the eventual victor, for the throne in 1292. Bruce now seized his chance and was crowned king at Scone on Palm Sunday 1306.

The early days did not bode well. Defeat near Perth saw him disappear into the western Highlands with a handful of loyal supporters. He was last seen leaving Kintyre in September, bound for his legendary encounter with a spider in a cave we know not where. When he reappeared in 1307, he shrewdly adopted a 'scorched-earth' tactic against the aggressor, resisting the temptation to fight a pitched battle but instead ordering his men to recapture the royal castles held by the English and demolish them so that they could no

Stirling Castle: The mighty royal castle overlooks two major battlefields – Stirling Bridge (September 1297), where William Wallace defeated Edward I of England's army, and Bannock-burn (June 1314), where King Robert Bruce overwhelmed Edward II.

King Robert Bruce: The equestrian statue of Robert Bruce stands over the battlefield of Bannockburn. The battle did not end the bloody Wars of Independence, but it did win for Bruce the unqualified support of the Scots as their sovereign king, after years of internecine rivalry with the Balliols.

Linlithgow Palace, West Lothian: The majestic palace of the Royal Stewarts was begun in the reign of James I (1406-37) and completed in the reign of James VI (1567-1625). The royal family used Linlithgow as an elegant 'pleasure palace'. The queens especially liked its tranquillity and fresh air. James V (1512), his daughter Mary, Queen of Scots (1542), and James VI's daughter, Elizabeth of Bohemia, 'the Winter Queen' (1596), were all born here.

longer be of practical use. By the summer of 1314 only mighty Stirling Castle was left in the enemy's hands, and by then Bruce felt strong enough to engage them in battle. His defeat of Edward II at Bannockburn, near Stirling, on Midsummer's Day 1314 ranks amongst the world's greatest battle victories.

For Bruce, Bannockburn was the defining moment in his reign. When he passed peacefully away near Dumbarton 15 years later, his position as king was unassailable. Yet his death was the signal for renewed English aggression, and soon the country was plunged into a second War of Independence. For 20 more years the struggle went on, during which Bruce's son, David II, battled with John Balliol's son, Edward, for the throne. Only with David II's return from captivity in England in 1357 can the Wars of Independence be truly said to have ended.

THE ROYAL STEWARTS

David II died childless in 1371 and Bruce's grandson, Robert the Stewart, became Robert II, the first of the royal Stewarts. The dynasty lasted for over three centuries. During that time, three of its monarchs died fighting the English (James II, IV and V), two were murdered by their own nobles (James I and III), two were beheaded (Mary and Charles I), and two were forced into exile

What's in a Name ?

Did you know... that the forebears of Wallace and Bruce weren't Scots? The name Wallace comes from 'le Waleys', literally 'the Welshman', whilst Bruce's father lived mostly in England, on his manor at Tottenham.

(Charles II and James VII). It reads as one long tale of woe, but it was far from so.

The splendid royal palaces at Falkland, Linlithgow and Stirling, and the rich court music of Robert Carver, testify to their majesty. Two historical achievements also stand out. In 1468, Scotland grew to its present extent when James III acquired Orkney and Shetland from the king of Norway; whilst in 1603 the unthinkable happened when James VI became also James I of England, through his descent from James IV and Margaret Tudor, 'the marriage of the thistle and the rose'. How Edward I would have hated that day!

MARY, QUEEN OF SCOTS

However, it is the short, ill-starred reign of Mary, Queen of Scots that holds our attention 400 years on, perhaps because it has all the ingredients of a great novel – romance, intrigue, tragedy. She was thrice married and thrice widowed, she never saw her father, James V, barely saw her son, James VI, miscarried of twins whilst a prisoner of her own lords, and ended her life on the executioner's block. What a life! Yet Mary's reign, turbulent though it was for her personally, was of little significance for Scotland as a whole. The most important event, the Protestant Reformation, took place in 1560 before she began to rule in person.

Execution of Mary, Queen of Scots: On 24 July 1567, at Lochleven Castle, Scotland, Mary was compelled to abdicate her throne. On 8 February 1587, at Fotheringhay Castle, England, she was executed. She was just 44 years old.

St Andrews Cathedral, Fife:
St Andrews was Scotland's premier cathedral city until the Protestant Reformation of 1560 brought about its downfall.

Mary Stewart was born in 1542 at Linlithgow Palace. Within a week she was queen. Henry VIII of England, spying an opportunity to seize the Scottish throne, proposed that Mary marry his son, Edward. He sent his army to do the wooing – the so-called 'War of the Rough Wooing'.

James IV

Did you know... that James IV's severed head, still sporting its shock of red hair and beard, was last seen on a mantelpiece in a London house around 1600? The king's bloodied corpse had been taken to Sheen Abbey, Surrey, after Flodden in 1513, but at the Dissolution of the Monasteries in the 1530s it was unceremoniously disposed of.

The Scots were not persuaded by such bullying and in 1548 smuggled little Mary to France. There she grew into an elegant lady, and in 1558 married the Dauphin, François. Then tragedy struck. Her father-in-law, Henri II, and husband died in quick succession, and Mary, queen of France for barely 18 months, was a widow. She returned home in August 1561.

Mary's short personal reign as queen of Scots was tempestuous, though her troubles were not entirely of her making. The Scottish Reformation began before her return from France. But Mary's own faults and misjudgements proved disastrous. Her Catholic leanings troubled her nobles and led to heated exchanges with John Knox, the fiery Protestant preacher. Her second marriage, to Lord Darnley in 1565, went horribly wrong, firstly when her Italian secretary and alleged lover, David Riccio, was murdered, then with the death in mysterious circumstances of Darnley himself. By now Mary was besotted by the earl of Bothwell, and soon after risking her health and reputation by riding across the bleak Border country to visit him at Hermitage Castle, they married.

Mary's dalliance with Bothwell proved her undoing and she was arrested by her nobles in 1567 and imprisoned in Lochleven Castle. There, on 24 July, she was compelled to abdicate in favour of her son, Prince James. His birth, in Edinburgh Castle in June 1566, was the one ray of sunshine in an otherwise stormy reign.

Mary eventually escaped her watery prison and fled to England, where she endured another 20 years as a virtual prisoner of her cousin, Queen Elizabeth. Finally, in 1587, Elizabeth, wearying of the continuing intrigue surrounding Mary, ordered her execution. Mary Queen of Scots became a legend the moment the executioner's axe severed her head from her body, at Fotheringhay Castle on Wednesday 8 February.

UNION OF THE CROWNS

When Elizabeth of England died in 1603, James VI became James I of England also. But the Union of the Crowns proved no panacea for the nation's ills and the 17th century was as troubled as any before. Religion in particular set king against country, clan against clan, family against family. Among the victims was James VI's successor Charles I, who was executed

James VI & I: When James VI of Scotland became James I of England as well, he assumed the title Rex Britanniae 'King of Great Britain'. The first step towards the creation of the United Kingdom had been taken.

by the English in 1649. But it was the Scots who first quarrelled with Charles when, in 1637, they protested at the introduction of the Book of Common Prayer. The National Covenant of 1638 fanned the flames of civil war.

Civil war was followed by Oliver Cromwell's invasion of 1650 and ten years of rule from England. Charles II, the last monarch crowned in Scotland, returned to his throne in 1660 only to reopen old religious wounds. The conflict between king and covenanter came to be known as the 'Killing Time' on account of the untold numbers who died. Charles' death in 1685, and the flight of his Catholic brother, James VII and II, in 1688 failed to stem the blood.

When the Protestant William and Mary were proclaimed joint sovereigns in 1689, Jacobitism (from 'Jacobus', Latin for James) was born. The 'Killing Time', though, continued, the most infamous event being 'the massacre of Glencoe' in the early hours of 13 February 1692 when 38 men, women and children of Clan Donald were murdered by Redcoats from Fort William.

Urquhart Castle, Loch Ness: (above) This defensive stronghold was in use until its destruction in the 17th century.

Glencoe, Argyll: (opposite) The infamous massacre took place in 'the narrow glen' in February 1692.

The Scottish Calendar

Did you know... it was James VI who changed the calendar to the one we are familiar with today? In 1600 he ordered that the Scottish calendar year begin on 1 January, and not on 25 March, the traditional start-date. England followed suit 150 years later!

Eighteenth-Century Scotland

Glenfinnan & Loch Shiel, Inverness-shire: The overthrow of James VII & II, the last Stuart king, in 1688 led to five separate uprisings by the Jacobites to regain their lost throne – in 1689, 1708, 1715, 1719 and 1745. The famous '45 began here in Glenfinnan when 'Bonnie Prince Charlie', James VII & II's grandson, raised his father's royal standard. It ended nine months later on the bloody battlefield of Culloden.

A UNITED KINGDOM

In January 1707, Parliament, meeting in Edinburgh, passed its final statute, the Act of Union. Scotland now merged with England to create the United Kingdom of Great Britain. Henceforth, the British Parliament would meet in London.

The Act of Union may have united the two nations but it brought great division in Scotland. The embers of Jacobitism were fanned into life once more and in 1708 James VIII, the 'Pretender', almost succeeded in landing an army on the Fife coast. The accession of the Elector of Hanover as George I in 1714 prompted another rising, which might well have succeeded had its commander, the earl of Mar, not been so inept. In 1716, with an army twice the size of George I's, he contrived to fight out a desultory draw at Sheriffmuir, near Stirling, and fled into exile soon after. The best chance the Stewarts had of reclaiming the throne had gone.

BONNIE PRINCE CHARLIE AND THE '45

In 1745, a boat beached on Eriskay, in the Western Isles. First ashore was a 25-year-old gentleman rejoicing in the name of Charles Edward Louis John Casimir Silvester Xavier Maria Stewart.

We know him better as 'Bonnie Prince Charlie', son of the 'Pretender'.

The first months of the '45 rising were momentous. On 19 August Prince Charles raised his father's standard at the head of Loch Shiel, near Fort William. By mid September he was captivating the ladies with his charm amid the grand surroundings of Holyroodhouse, ancient palace of the Stewarts in Edinburgh, and in the early morning of 21 September, he led his army to victory over George II's 'Redcoats' at Prestonpans, east of the capital. On 15 November, they crossed into England, and by 4 December had reached Derby. There, beside the Trent, with London at their mercy, they halted. The truth was slowly dawning on the would-be Prince Regent. The anticipated Jacobite support had not materialised on the long march south; neither had the anticipated French invasion of southern England. The Jacobite leaders, most of them from the Scottish Highlands, felt vulnerable. Carry on to London, or beat a tactical withdrawal? They voted to go home.

And there at Culloden, east of Inverness, on 16 April 1746, the remnants of Bonnie Prince Charlie's army fell before the Redcoats' guns. Over one thousand men, mostly

Queen Anne receiving a copy of The Treaty of Union: The creation of the United Kingdom of Great Britain in 1707 was a defining moment in Scotland's and England's history.

The Act of Union

Did you know... just 150 Scots, out of a population of over 1 million Scots, voted to enter the Union with England in 1707 – 10 dukes, 3 marquesses, 75 earls, 17 viscounts and 45 lords? Of the rest of the people, three out of every four were classed as peasants, with barely any rights at all.

The Battle of Culloden: Morier, the official war artist for George II, depicts the decisive moment in the bloody battle when the kilted clansmen of Clan Chattan engaged with redcoats from Barrell's Regiment. Morier titled his painting 'An incident in the Rebellion of 1745'. Some incident! Over a thousand dead on the battlefield, and the end of the dream for the House of Stewart of regaining the British throne.

Highlanders, who had worn the blue bonnet and white cockade with pride, lay dead or dying on the windswept moor. The last pitched battle fought on British soil effectively ended the Stewart dream of reclaiming the throne.

NORTH BRITAIN

Culloden was emphatically not a war between Scotland and England. Rather, it was the culmination of a bloody civil war in which nationality played only a minor part. Jacobitism was a confusing flag of convenience for people with differing agendas – for those who simply wished to see the House of Stewart return to the throne, for those who sought to overthrow Presbyterianism, and for those who despised the Union for whatever reason. Highlander was set against Lowlander, Scot against Scot;

even members of the same family fought each other that April day.

Time, though, is a great healer, and the faltering start to the new Great Britain slowly gave way to optimism. By degrees the economic benefits of union began to be felt, and Scots found new energies and dynamism. Glasgow emerged as the leading town in the west, thanks to the growing tobacco and sugar trade with England's American colonies. Loss of national identity was but a small price to pay for prosperity.

The very name 'Scotland' itself came under threat after the Union. The London government did its utmost to promote the concept of 'North Britain' in an attempt to devalue the contribution of the junior partner. They never once thought to use the phrase 'South Britain' in place of England! Such arrogance merely made the Scots more determined to succeed, which they did with an emphatic flourish in the years to come.

SCOTLAND'S 'AGE OF ENLIGHTENMENT'

Later 18th-century Scotland was a dazzling period of sustained intellectual thought and artistic creativity that had the eyes of the world gazing in admiration on this poor land on the edge of Europe. Even the great Voltaire proclaimed: 'It is to Edinburgh that we must look for our intellectual tastes'.

The 'stars' of the Enlightenment were mostly university professors, kirk ministers and lawyers – 'teachers, preachers and pleaders'; men of the calibre of David Hume, Scotland's greatest philosopher, whose profound scepticism made him

question the fundamental concepts on which all knowledge and belief is founded. He put the 'light' into the Enlightenment, and his influence was profound. Around him glowed such luminaries as Adam Smith, whose *Inquiry into the Nature and Causes of the Wealth of Nations*, published in 1776, established economics as a social science; James Hutton, the father of modern geology; the pioneering James Watt with his steam engine; the groundbreaking civil engineers Thomas Telford and John Rennie; William Adam and son Robert in the architectural sphere; and creative artists such as Henry Raeburn, Robert Burns and Walter Scott – the list is almost endless. The century also saw Scotland give to the world a remarkable number of 'firsts', including the first steam engine, the first post office and the first savings bank. For a small country, Scotland's contribution to the world has been immense.

Edinburgh New Town: The broad streets and graceful crescents of Edinburgh's Georgian New Town, created during Scotland's 'Age of Enlightenment', reflected the Scottish capital's status as the United Kingdom's 'second city'. Many stars of the Enlightenment were either born here, or made it their home.

David Hume: Born and bred in Edinburgh, Hume was one of the greatest philosophers of his time, and the leading figure of Scotland's 'Age of Enlightenment'.

Late 18th-century Rural Scene: The Edinburgh-born artist Alexander Naysmith began as a portrait painter but his passion for the natural world, and man's relationship to it, took over – as demonstrated in this contemporary pastoral study. He is now known as the father of Scottish landscape painting.

Robert Burns: Scotland's greatest poet inspired not just the people of his own time but all subsequent generations too. In 2009, Scots from all across the world celebrated the 250th anniversary of his birth with the 'Year of Homecoming'.

ROBERT BURNS

Robert Burns was born into poverty in an 'auld clay biggin' in Alloway in 1759, laboured as ploughboy, flax-dresser, farmer and exciseman, and died still a pauper in a meagre rented room in Dumfries in 1796. His was a short, and sometimes sad life, and yet he contrived through his poetry to enrich the lives of so many, not just his contemporaries, and not just Scots, but people yesterday and today and the world over.

Burns wrote over 80 poems, and composed or collected over 200 songs. 'Tam o' Shanter', perhaps his most well-known poem, was written in a single day. Burns's poetry reaches into the hearts of us all. They show a humour, a warmth, a tenderness; they reveal a contempt for those in authority; they rail against injustice, and speak up for the defenceless

individual; they weave words into wonderful tales that hold the child in us in thrall to this day.

But above all Burns' poetry tells of love. It was love that first brought the 14-year-old 'heaven-taught ploughboy' into poetry, and love that sustained him throughout his brief, troubled life. Some of the finest love-poems in the English language are his, among them 'Ae Fond Kiss' and 'Ye Banks and Braes'.

As Dante is to Italy, and Yeats to Ireland, so Burns is to Scotland – her greatest poet. And yet this simple Ayrshire 'lad o' pairts' is greater even than that, for he is revered internationally. As every 25 January arrives, men and women around the world 'pipe in' the haggis and raise

a glass of whisky to his 'immortal memory'. He wrote in his native Scots' tongue, but his words were universal.

AGRICULTURAL REVOLUTION

The Scot of 1800 would scarcely have recognised the Scotland of a century earlier. Not only had the Union indelibly altered the political landscape; the physical landscape too had changed out of all recognition, thanks to the agricultural revolution. Gone were the broad, sweeping rigs that had existed for centuries, to be replaced by neat fields enclosed by hedges and stone dykes.

With agricultural improvement came technical innovation. The 'pocket-handkerchief' appearance of the Lowland landscape could not have been achieved with the old tools, the simple spade and the unwieldy plough pulled by 12 oxen. Newfangled machines were invented by 'enlightened' Scots: James Small, from Berwickshire, who designed a swing-plough drawn by just two horses, Andrew Meikle, from East Lothian, who perfected the threshing machine, and the Dundonian, Patrick Bell, who invented a reaper whose motion still beats at the heart of every modern combine-harvester.

But the whole process was not without pain. The creation of single-farm tenancies made many a tenant landless. Forced evictions became commonplace across the Lowlands. The first resistance to the new order came as early as 1724 with the Levellers' Revolt in Galloway, in protest at the creation of large 'black cattle' farms. By the end of the century Highlanders too were taking matters into their own hands, this time about the proliferation of sheep farms. In 1792

Tobermory, Isle of Mull: The 'capital' of Mull, with its brightly painted buildings lining the quayside, was created in the 1780s, at the same time as Edinburgh's New Town. The British Fisheries Society, built it to provide much needed employment for Highlanders in the aftermath of Culloden.

The Kilmarnock Edition

Did you know... Robert Burns planned to emigrate to Jamaica in 1786? Having secured a job as overseer on a sugar plantation, he set about raising the finance by publishing his first anthology: *Poems Chiefly in the Scottish Dialect*. The Kilmarnock Edition made Burns instantly popular and he decided to remain in his native land.

Clearance Township, Isle of Raasay: The clearance of Raasay was typical of the last phase of Highland Clearances. In 1843, MacLeod of Raasay, driven to bankruptcy, sold out and emigrated to Tasmania. Three years later a destructive potato blight wrought famine on the crofters, and the new owner turned to sheep-farming instead. In 1852 he 'cleared' several townships, and two boat-loads of emigrants left for a new life in Australia.

crofters in Easter Ross rounded up all the woolly creatures they could lay their hands on – 10,000 of them – and herded them south. They would have driven them out of the Highlands altogether had they not been intercepted by soldiers from the Black Watch Regiment. The year 1792 still lives on in Highland folklore as *Bliadhna Nan Caorach*, 'the Year of the Sheep'. But worse was to follow.

THE HIGHLAND CLEARANCES

The infamous Highland Clearances took place during the first half of the 19th century. But well before then, crofters had been leaving their homes in search of a better life. Some went south to the

Central Belt in search of work, others chose emigration, mostly to the wide-open spaces of Canada.

In those days it hadn't been in the landlords' interest to remove them, for they needed cheap labour to help them harvest seaweed for the booming kelp industry. But war with Napoleon's France ruined that enterprise, and landlords had little option but to look for alternatives; they opted for sheep-farming. But flocks of sheep only need a few shepherds – and so the crofters had to go.

The notorious 'clearance' of thousands of families from Strathnaver, in Sutherland, between 1807 and 1821 is engrained on the national consciousness as the grossest act of inhumanity ever perpetrated by a landlord on his tenantry. Whole townships were uprooted from the land their ancestors had worked from time immemorial and transplanted to the storm-lashed north coast. Those grim years are scarred with harrowing accounts of dreadful hurt inflicted on a cowed and terrified people.

But whilst we must never forget those awful events, it is important that we put them in perspective. As Patrick Sellar, the Duke of Sutherland's factor, was wielding his stick of eviction, his employers were dangling the carrot of inducement in front of their tenants' noses in an effort to persuade them to leave the glens of their own accord. The Sutherland Estates invested substantial sums of money in coal mines, a whisky distillery, harbours and fish-curing stations, inns and fine houses.

The Duke and Duchess of Sutherland were not alone. Across the Highlands, landlords were wrestling with the problem of overpopulation in similar ways, helped by government grants and enterprises, such as Thomas Telford's great Caledonian Canal, opened in 1822.

For a while all went reasonably well. Then disaster struck. In 1846-7, a destructive blight struck the potato crop on which the people were so dependent. It brought untold misery on the families toiling on their meagre patches of ground. Forced eviction was now the only answer. And so they went in their tens of thousands. Whole communities were plucked from the shore, like the seaweed they had once lifted, dropped into ships and despatched to Canada, Australia and New Zealand. 20,000 Highlanders sailed for Canada alone. Just as many drifted south to the factories and mines of the Clyde. The age-old bond between crofter and land, between tenant and landlord, was broken, and an eerie silence descended on the straths and glens.

But the question remains: was there a more humane solution to the problem of overpopulation? What would have happened had the crofters been left to go on scratching a living from smaller and smaller plots of land? One thing is sure – there remains no greater stain on the pages of Highland history than the infamous 'Highland Clearances'.

The Last of the Clan: Faed's poignant depiction of the Highland Clearances was exhibited at the Royal Academy in 1865, shortly after the last of the clearances had taken place. The remaining members of a clan stand forlornly on the shore awaiting their turn to leave their homeland. Whether they sailed south to the factories on the Clyde or emigrated to foreign climes we shall never know.

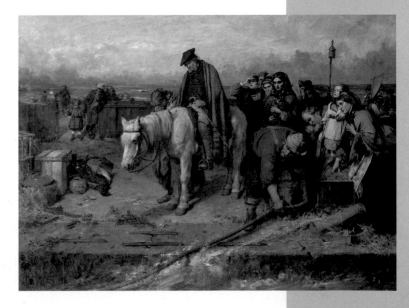

Industrial Scotland

Cowlairs Erecting Shop, Glasgow, c 1900: Cowlairs engineering works helped make Glasgow the 'boiler house' of the British Empire. By 1900, Clydeside was exporting heavy engineering products, such as the railway locomotives rolling off Cowlairs' production line, all over the world, making 'Clyde-built' a byword for quality and price. But the wages paid to the workers for producing the economic miracle were pitifully low, brewing up trouble for the future.

WORKSHOP OF EMPIRE

In 1821 less than half the population lived in the Glasgow area. A century later, that figure had risen to well over 80 per cent. During that time, Scotland was transformed from a predominantly rural land to one of the most industrialised countries on earth – 'the workshop of the British Empire – with Glasgow its undisputed 'second city' after London. But how?

In 1801, a seam of rock was discovered in a coalmine near Glasgow –

blackband ironstone. James Beaumont Neilson, inventor of the 'hot blast' smelting process, found that 'Blackband' and 'King Coal' made a powerful double-act, and within 30 years Glasgow had become the centre of the world's iron industry, with over 100 ironworks in and around Glasgow belching out pig iron and palls of smoke in equal measure. So fiery was the sky at night over Coatbridge that one sightseer told of there being 'no worse place out of hell'.

The output of the new ironworks, and later the steelworks, spawned new engineering industries, as enterprising Scots realised the potential. Everything from modest machine tools to monstrous steam engines were soon rolling off the production lines and into domestic and world markets. The phrase 'Clyde-built' became synonymous with quality as Scottish engineering skills earned respect across the globe. From that time Scotsmen have often figured

Jute weaving shed of Hardie & Smith's Baltic Works, Dundee: In stark contrast to the male-dominated heavy industries on Clydeside, Dundee's industrial jute-spinning and weaving workforce was overwhelmingly female.

as canny engineers in works of fiction, from Kipling's M'Andrew to Star Trek's 'Scottie'.

One of the most significant new products to emerge was the railway locomotive. No sooner had the 'iron horse' been invented in the 1820s (by an Englishman, George Stephenson, but only made possible through the inventiveness of James Watt, from Greenock, who had previously perfected the steam engine) than the first locomotive-driven railway in Scotland was operating, between Glasgow and Garnkirk to its east. Soon steam 'locos' capable of reaching frightening speeds of 30 mph were rocketing past the snail-paced boats on the canals, and threatening the stagecoach for supremacy as the main means of public transport. By 1842 the first intercity service was running between Glasgow and Edinburgh, and by 1850 trains were puffing over the Border to England. Another knot in the Union was tied.

Scottish locomotives were shipped all over the world, transported to the furthest reaches of the Empire and beyond in that other great engineering product of the Clyde, the steamship. From the day in 1812 when the passenger steamer *Comet* sailed out from Port Glasgow to herald the world's first commercial steamship service, the Clyde's name as one of the world's great shipbuilding centres was assured. By 1900, one half of the United Kingdom's marine engines and a fifth of the world's ships – cargo vessels, liners and battleships – were sliding down into the

Launching of the Queen Elizabeth at John Brown's shipyard, Clydebank: Producing huge ocean-going vessels such as the S.S. Queen Elizabeth was one of the core heavy industries on Clydeside. By 1914, one third of the U.K.'s ships slipped down the river's many slipways and out onto the oceans of the world.

Female herring gutters at Peterhead, c 1900: Fishing became a major industry in 19th-century Scotland, and by 1850 the herring fleet numbered in the thousands. Many men and women would follow the herring migration around the Scottish coast and down into England during the summer months, when the men fished, and the woment processed the catch.

Clyde's murky waters and onto the world's oceans.

But whilst Clydesiders sweated in the locomotive works, or cheered as their ships glided down the slipways, Scots elsewhere continued to work the land and labour in traditional industries. In 1815, nine out of every ten working Scots were employed in textiles. In Ayrshire they specialised in lace, in Paisley silk shawls, in the Border towns woollen knitwear and tweeds, in Dunfermline fine linen, and in Dundee jute – one of the three 'Js' (the others being 'Jam' and 'Journalism') for which Dundee is famous. So important was jute to the town on the Tay that they called it 'Juteopolis'.

But times were changing here as everywhere. Competition from overseas, coupled with wars here, there and everywhere disrupting supplies and markets, forced the industry to cut its costs or perish. The answer was to employ cheaper labour. Unlike heavy

engineering, which required plenty of muscle, cotton-spinning, lace-making and thread-weaving were just as easily done by women and children. By 1880, two out of every three workers in an industry employing over 100,000 people were women and children. In Dundee, almost the entire workforce was female. Little surprise then to learn that it was in Dundee that women first took formal strike action when the Dundee and District Mill and Factory Operatives' Union 'downed tools' in 1885.

At the outset of the industrial revolution in the 1780s, Scotland was a land where power and privilege were the preserve of the few, servility and suffering the sad lot of the many. Now, a century on, the working class was arming itself for a tilt at the twin windmills of political democracy and workers' rights.

STATE AND SOCIETY

Plentiful labour helped create Scotland's economic miracle, but working conditions were mostly appalling – six days a week, 14 hours a day, with two extra days off a year if you were lucky. A jingle popular with Fife ploughmen in 1903 ran: 'Six days shalt thou labour and do all you are able; On the Sabbath-day wash the horses' legs and tidy up the stable'. The excessively long hours applied equally to women and children as they did to men.

If labour was plentiful, then life was cheap. Take coal. In Victorian Scotland,

800 men were killed or seriously injured on average every year, 207 men and boys in a single incident at the Blantyre pit in 1877, Scotland's biggest mining disaster. Not for nothing was it said that there was 'blood on every ton of coal'.

As if spending 14 hours a day in appalling working conditions wasn't bad enough, spare a thought for those workers as they returned to their homes of an evening. Edinburgh's medieval 'high-rise' tenements had long had an unenviable reputation for crampedness and inadequate sanitation, but they were as nothing compared to the new tenement jungles rising up around the Clyde. The 1861 Census exposes the stark reality: 34 per cent of all homes with just one room (the 'single end'), 37 per cent with just two rooms (the 'but-and-ben'), and 1 per cent of families living in rooms without any windows!

The problem was worst in Glasgow simply because of the monstrous growth of the place from provincial cathedral city to big-time metropolis. Disease and death were frequent visitors to the crowded wynds and closes. Over 4000 people were killed at one fell swoop during the cholera epidemic of 1853. The disaster prompted the city fathers to build the Loch Katrine Water Works. In breeding grounds such as these, little wonder that one child in five never got the chance to celebrate its first birthday, or that half of the city's wains died before they were five.

The arrival of Highlanders removed by the 'Clearances' simply exacerbated an existing problem; the arrival of the Irish added a new ingredient to the already volatile situation – sectarianism – for those crossing the Irish Sea were both Catholics and Protestants. Irish immigrants had begun to have an impact on Scottish society before 1800, mainly as seasonal workers making the short sea-crossing to eke out their paltry wages by labouring on Lowland farms and in factories across the Central Belt. By 1830, 'ghettos' of Catholic and Protestant immigrants had begun to appear. But in the wake of the great famine of 1846, a massive tidal wave of immigrants swept up the Clyde, more than 30,000 in four months in 1847.

Close, No. 46 Salt-market, Glasgow c 1868: The tenants pose for a staged photograph. But behind the smiles lurk some appalling statistics. Illness, disease and death were frequent visitors to Glasgow's overcrowded closes. One child in five never reached their first birthday, and over 4,000 people died in one fell swoop during the cholera epidemic of 1853.

New Lanark:
The textile village nestling below the dramatic Falls of Clyde, established by David Dale in 1785, employed a 2,000-strong workforce. Dale's son-in-law, the enlightened Robert Owen, became manager and revolutionised the mills with social reforms, including banning child labour.

day, it was the State that took the initiative. Despite vociferous opposition from powerful sections of society, including town councils and the Church of Scotland who resented growing interference from 'Big Brother', government commissions were set up to investigate and report on a whole raft of issues, from child-employment to public health and housing. Legislation followed, slowly but steadily. As early as 1833, Althorp's Act set a minimum age of nine for children working in cotton mills, and limited the working day of under-13s to eight hours. The 1842 Mining Act put an end to the practice of women and children being sent down the pit.

Employers weren't the only ones to cavil at this unwarranted intervention in their affairs. The Church of Scotland too was concerned at this growing State interference. For three centuries, kirk sessions across Scotland had toiled long and hard to help the needy in society, and educate its young children. Now the State was threatening to intervene. But it was an unseemly row over patronage, the right to appoint ministers to parishes, that led directly to the Disruption of 1843, when two-fifths of the clergy and a third of their congregations 'walked out' to form the Free Church of Scotland, independent of the State. The result was that the squabbling rump of clerics left behind lost much of its credibility, powerless to stop the State taking over responsibility

By 1850, Glasgow was home to 10 per cent of all of Britain's Irish immigrants. All were starved and destitute; most were Catholics. The brewing resentment soon bubbled up into open conflict. A century and a half later and Scotland still bears the scars of that bitter rivalry.

The increasingly dire situation of the urban working class could not continue if Scotland's economic miracle was to continue. Something had to be done. Ironically, in an age when laissez-faire, 'leave well alone', was the order of the for the two main planks in the Kirk's mission since the Reformation – poor relief and elementary education. By World War I, compulsory education for all five to 14-year-olds, free school meals and 'nit ladies' had become part-and-parcel of Scottish life.

LABOUR MOBILISED

The growing State intervention in the way Scots lived their lives was officially recognised in 1885 with the creation of the Scottish Office. The Duke of Richmond – the former aide-de-camp to the Duke of Wellington – was appointed Secretary of State. But in one vital area, that of workers' rights, there had scarcely been any progress at all. The arrival on the stage of someone far removed from the privileged world of Charles Henry, Duke of Richmond, changed all that. Cue James Keir Hardie.

By the time Keir Hardie stood for parliamentary election as an 'Independent Labour' candidate in 1888, a few concessions had been wrung out of the employers and the State. In 1868 the right to vote was extended to all urban male householders, adding another 100,000 names to the electoral roll drawn up in 1832. In 1885, their rural counterparts were added also, thereby enfranchising that other long-abused element in society, the crofters. Now, only 40 per cent of the male population remained without the vote – and all the women of course.

Hardie was born a Liberal, as were most of the working class. But the bloody events over the winter of 1886-7 changed all that, as the workers' hopes for improved pay and working conditions were cruelly dashed beneath the stamping hooves of the hussars' horses in the Blantyre miners' strike of 1886-7. From the moment Hardie helped found the Scottish Labour Party in Glasgow on 19 May 1888, the Liberal Party, in the ascendancy over their arch-rivals the Tories for most of the century, was forced onto the back foot. From the time he helped form the British Labour Party in 1900, Liberalism was forced onto the defensive across the United Kingdom as a whole.

But no sooner had the new century dawned than a far greater menace threatened the stability, even the very existence, of the United Kingdom. Liberal, Tory and Labour had all to put aside their differences to confront a new threat – Germany.

Forth Bridge: In March 1890, Edward Prince of Wales officially opened the new rail bridge spanning the Firth of Forth. John Fowler and Benjamin Baker's innovative cantilevered creation was soon being hailed as 'the eighth wonder of the world'. The awesome but elegant steel and stone structure, still very much in use, stands as a fitting memorial to the Victorian industrial miracle.

Twentieth-Century Scotland

THE GREAT WAR

Over 500,000 Scots fought in the Great War, a tenth of the population. One in four never made it back. As the troops left for Flanders shortly after war was declared on 4 August 1914, they said they'd be back by Christmas; little did they know it would be Christmas 1918.

The statistics of the slaughter are as stark as the rows of neat headstones in the war cemeteries. Mons 1914 – 1000 men of the 1st Royal Scots Fusiliers reduced to 70; Loos, September 1915 – most of the 15th Scottish Division lost in the opening minutes of the battle; Somme, July 1916 – an estimated 6300 casualties on the first day, including men from the Argyll and Sutherland, Cameron, Gordon and Seaforth Highlanders. And so on, and so on. And not just in Flanders, but on the beaches of Gallipoli, in Eastern Europe, the Near East and Egypt, on the high seas, and in an entirely new theatre, the air.

The eagerness with which young Scotsmen hurried to their nearest recruiting station in those first days overwhelms us who have the benefit of hindsight and know all too well

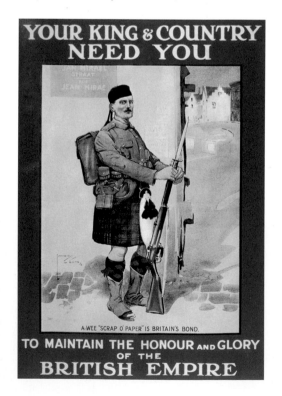

YOUR KING & COUNTRY NEED YOU

A WEE "SCRAP O' PAPER" IS BRITAIN'S BOND.

TO MAINTAIN THE HONOUR and GLORY OF THE BRITISH EMPIRE

what horrors were in store; for the 20,000 who queued outside Glasgow's Gallowgate office before that first August was out; for the Watsonians XV who enlisted en masse in Edinburgh's regiment, the Royal Scots; for the countless others who joined the 'pals' battalions, whole groups of men and boys from the same town, the same slums, all flocking to the same colours.

The Great War affected not only those who had to endure the carnage; it touched those left behind too. No one death was easy to accept, but the grieving can have been no more acute than in those communities who had bid farewell to their 'wee, hard men' of the 'pals' battalions, only to learn later that they had been gunned down almost as one. Over 500 men from Glasgow's Boys Brigade, who had helped form the 16th Highland Light Infantry in 1914, fell on the first morning of the Somme; many were from the same street.

The Great War was not without its good points. It brought a welcome respite for Clydeside's ailing heavy industries, and it brought too a truce in the political wrangling that had seen the recent emergence of the Labour Party and the Suffragette movement. Now everyone rolled up their collective sleeves and rallied round. As David Kirkwood, shop steward and 'Red Clydesider', later declared: 'I was too proud of the battles of the past to stand aside and see Scotland conquered.'

That feeling of pride in the past endured throughout the long and bitter struggle, and was finally rewarded with victorious peace on 11 November 1918.

AN UNEASY PEACE

The 'war to end wars' was over, but peace in Europe brought little peace to Scotland, particularly to the industrial heartland where, despite the hopes and expectations of those returning from the trenches, the misery continued. Scarcely was the war over than there was confrontation. In January 1919, 80,000

George Square, Glasgow, 31 January 1919: The 'Red Flag' flies above the cloth-capped workers striking for a 40-hour week. 'Bloody Friday' proved a turning-point in British political life, and in 1922 the Labour Party won its first General Election.

Edinburgh Ambush

Did you know... that Edinburgh was once attacked by a German Zeppelin? In April 1916, the airship appeared over Leith and proceeded to drop bombs on the city, killing several people. A few hit the Castle Rock but caused no damage to the ancient citadel.

Churchill Barriers, Orkney: *In WWI the sea-lanes into the Scapa Flow naval base were blocked by redundant merchant ships. But after the sinking of HMS* Royal Oak *in October 1939, Winston Churchill ordered they be sealed by concrete barriers.*

Ramsay MacDonald.

But the problems underlying Scotland's economy were profound. The monolithic heavy industries of the Clyde had become like huge dinosaurs, still casting their monstrous shadows over the land but increasingly unable to cope with the fast-changing world. 'Diversify or die'; most chose death. The result was recession and rising unemployment. By the time of the 'General Strike' of 1926, one in seven workers was idle. After the 'Wall Street Crash' of 1929, that figure had risen to as high as one in two in 'black spots' like Airdrie. The numbers emigrating grew too – 500,000 to the 'New World' in the 1920s alone. During the 'Great Depression' of the 1930s, the population drift to the south-east of England began in earnest.

In political circles thoughts turned once more to freedom from the English yoke. Home Rule had long been a plank of Liberal policy, but nothing had come of it. Now in the 1920s 'nationalism' was increasingly whispered abroad. In 1921, the Scots National League was formed, the body that in 1934 was recast as the Scottish National Party (SNP). 'I want for my part/ Only the little white rose of Scotland/That smells sharp and sweet/And breaks my

men walked out in support of a 40-hour week. Many headed to a rally in George Square. Prime Minister Lloyd George, fearful of a 'Bolshevist rising', ordered in the police. They called that day 'Bloody Friday'. But the struggle continued. At the following general election in 1922, Labour in Scotland won by a landslide; by 1924, it was in Government, under the leadership of Lossiemouth-born

heart', wrote Hugh MacDiarmid, founder member of the party.

Government did its best to alleviate the suffering and snuff out the unrest. Various Housing Acts led to wholesale slum clearances, and the building of new estates in the suburbs. Neat bungalows could be bought for £400, but they did say the ceilings were so low all you could eat for tea was a kipper! Even in the Highlands and Islands, the times were 'a-changing', as the traditional thatched 'blackhouses' made way for new lime-cemented 'white houses'. But one 'house' above all best articulates both the fears and aspirations of Scots in those pain-filled years of peace – St Andrew's House, Edinburgh, completed in 1939 for the Scottish Office, then still working out of Whitehall. But even as the Secretary of State, Colonel John Colville, was finalising the move of his 1300 staff

northward, the leader of another country was ordering his troops eastward into Poland. On 3 September 1939 Britain was once again at war with Germany.

WORLD WAR II

The war visited its wrath on Scotland just over a month after war was declared on 3 September 1939. In the early morning of 14 October, German U-boat *U-47* sneaked into the naval base at Scapa Flow, Orkney, and sent HMS *Royal Oak* and most of its 883 crew to the bottom. Two days later, Spitfires shot down the

Cinema City

Did you know... that Glasgow once had more cinemas than any other city in the world outside the USA? During the 1930s there were 114, hence Glasgow's nickname 'Cinema City'.

Finnieston Crane & Clyde Arc, Glasgow: *The old shipyards in Glasgow are being transformed into vibrant centres of entertainment and commerce. The innovative Clyde Arc, uniting the two banks of the river opened in 2006, and is known as the 'Squinty Bridge' by Glaswegians. The Finnieston Crane, erected in 1928, stands in the distance as a monument to Glasgows' industrial past.*

first German plane over East Lothian.

Scotland was directly affected as never before, from the threat of aerial bombardment and sea-borne invasion. Children were evacuated from the vulnerable cities before the bombs began to fall – most devastatingly on Clydebank over the nights of 13 and 14 March 1941, when over 1200 civilians were killed and 35,000 left homeless, from a population of 50,000.

In the face of such horrors, everyone wanted to 'do their bit'. Young lads swarmed down into the 384 coalmines then operating in Scotland (not one pit now remains), whilst others joined home units such as the Home Guard and the Women's Land Army. Scotland became a

fortress as concrete pillboxes sprouted up around the coast, and a giant aircraft carrier; RAF Prestwick became the busiest airport in the world as USAF Flying Fortresses flew in and out en route to Germany.

But wars were fought and won mostly in the front line, and World War II was truly a 'world war'. Scotsmen and women found themselves operating in every theatre – Europe, Asia and the Far East, on and under the oceans and in the skies. Their exploits would fill an entire library. Suffice it to record here that over 58,000 Scots gave their lives for their country, until at last the church bells, silent for the duration, rang out in celebration of victory on 8 May 1945.

SCOTLAND TODAY

Scotland has changed out of all recognition since World War II. No more do reeking furnaces light up the night sky, or black-faced miners emerge blinking into the daylight. Few are the ships being launched into the water, and even fewer the crans of fish being lifted out of it. We weren't sure what would replace them, if anything, in those difficult post-war years. They were our traditional industries, they had 'ay been'. That is why we tried so hard to cling on to them.

But we didn't know then what we know now – that vast oil-wells lurked beneath the North Sea, that a tiny atom could generate energy sufficient to power whole cities, that a plastic 'chip' smaller than your thumbnail would transform all our lives. Where colliery pit-heads and factory chimneys once loomed, today shiny new electronics industries thrive; Scotland's Central Belt is now known by another name – 'Silicon Glen'.

Scotland, though, has retained its distinctiveness, its national identity, despite the global 'village' we inhabit. It never became 'North Britain', and it won't become 'North-West Europe' either. It remains emphatically Scottish, with a cultural identity forged over thousands of years.

Oil Platforms in the Cromarty Firth: In the 1970s, a new industry came to Scotland's, and Britain's, rescue – North Sea oil. By 1980 giant rigs such as these were helping to pump £5 billion into the nation's coffers.

The Scottish Parliament Building, Holyrood, Edinburgh: In 1997 Scotland achieved devolution from Westminster. The first elections to the new Scottish Parliament – the first to sit in 292 years - were held in 1999, and a new parliament building was opened in 2004.

Chronology of Scotland

BC

11,000	Last Ice Age ends.
9,000	First humans arrive.
6,000	Britain physically separates from Europe.
3,100	Skara Brae Neolithic village built.
2,900	Maes Howe tomb built.
2,200	First metals appear – the 'Bronze Age'.
700	Iron appears – the 'Iron Age'.
200	First brochs built.

AD

79	Rome invades Scotland.
83	Roman legionaries defeat Caledonian tribes at Mons Graupius.
142	Rome builds Antonine Wall, between Forth and Clyde.
297	First mention of Picts in historical records.
367	Picts and Scots raid beyond Hadrian's Wall.
450	'Latinus Stone', Scotland's oldest Christian memorial, erected at Whithorn.
563	St Columba arrives in Argyll and establishes monastery on Iona.
597	St Columba dies on Iona.
600	Northern Britons defeated by Angles at Catterick.
638	Angles capture Din Eidyn from Britons and rename it Edinburgh.
685	Angles defeated by Picts at Nechtansmere.
794	First Viking raid on Iona.
843	Gaels and Picts unite under Kenneth mac Alpin to form kingdom of Scotland.
871	Vikings capture British strong-hold of Dumbarton Rock.
904	Scots defeat Vikings in Strathearn.
954	Scots capture Edinburgh from Anglo-Saxons.
1018	Scots defeat English at Carham.
1057	King Macbeth killed at Lumphanan.
1093	Malcolm III 'Canmore' killed fighting Normans in Northumberland.
1266	Treaty of Perth sees Hebrides returned to Scotland.
1295	Pact signed between Scotland and France – the 'Auld Alliance'.
1296	Edward I invades. The Wars of Independence start.
1297	William Wallace leads Scots to victory at Stirling Bridge.
1305	William Wallace executed in London.
1306	Robert Bruce enthroned as king at Scone.
1314	Bruce defeats Edward II of England at Bannockburn.
1320	Scots send letter to Pope John XXII – the 'Declaration of Arbroath' – pleading for their right to sovereign independence.
1349	The 'Black Death comes to Scotland.
1371	Robert, the High Stewart, becomes Robert II – first of the Stewart dynasty.
1412	St Andrews University founded, Scotland's first.
1468	Orkney and Shetland pass from Norway to Scotland.
1482	Berwick-upon-Tweed ceded to England for good.
1500	Population estimated to be around 500,000.
1508	First Scottish books printed.
1513	James IV and 5000 Scots – 'the flower of Scotland' – killed at Flodden.
1560	Parliament passes Act of Reformation. First General Assembly meets.
1567	Mary, Queen of Scots forced to abdicate.
1572	John Knox, 'architect' of the Reformation, dies in Edinburgh.
1587	Mary Queen of Scots executed at Fotheringhay Castle, England.
1600	1 January adopted as start of calendar year (previously 25 March).
1603	James VI becomes James I of England also – 'Union of the Crowns'.
1638	National Covenant signed.
1650	Cromwell invades Scotland and wins battle of Dunbar.
1663	Non-conforming ministers expelled from Kirk. Start of the 'Killing Time'.
1689	James VII deposed and replaced by William and Mary. First Jacobite Rising.
1692	Massacre of Glencoe.
1695	Bank of Scotland established.
1700	Population reaches 1 million.
1707	Treaty of Union between Scotland and England – 'Union of the Parliaments'.
1708	James VIII & III ('The Pretender') leads abortive second Jacobite Rising.
1715	Third Jacobite Rising follows coronation of Elector of Hanover as George I.
1719	Fourth Jacobite Rising ends in defeat at battle of Glenshiel.
1725	General Wade arrives in Scotland and begins to build military roads.
1727	Royal Bank of Scotland founded. Last Scottish witch burned, at Dornoch.

Year	Event	Year	Event
1744	Honourable Society of Edinburgh Golfers plays first 'medal' on Leith Links.	1914	World War I begins.
1746	Last Jacobite Rising ends in defeat for Bonnie Prince Charlie at Culloden.	1915	217 Royal Scots killed in train crash near Gretna.
1759	Carron Ironworks founded. Robert Burns born in Alloway.	1916	6,000 Scots killed on first day of the Somme. Zeppelin bombs Edinburgh.
1764	James Watt perfects his steam engine in Glasgow.	1918	World War I ends. Women given the right to vote.
1767	Foundation stone laid for Edinburgh's New Town.	1919	German Grand Fleet scuttled in Scapa Flow. Forestry Commission set up.
1776	Adam Smith publishes *Wealth of Nations*. David Hume, philosopher, dies.	1923	First radio stations set up in Glasgow and Aberdeen.
1790	Forth & Clyde Canal, the 'Great Canal', opens.	1924	Ramsay MacDonald becomes first Labour Prime Minister.
1792	Revolt in Strathoykel against sheep-farms. Robert Adam, architect, dies.	1926	General Strike. John Logie Baird transmits first television picture.
1796	Robert Burns dies in Dumfries.	1928	Sir Alexander Fleming discovers penicillin. First female Scots MP elected.
1799	Serfdom banned in coalmines and saltworks.	1930	36 islanders evacuated from St Kilda.
1801	Population exceeds 1.5 million.	1931	National Trust for Scotland founded.
1807	First of the 'Highland Clearances' begins on the Sutherland Estate.	1934	Scottish National Party formed.
1810	World's first savings bank opens at Ruthwell, Dumfriesshire.	1939	World War II begins. HMS *Royal Oak* sunk in Scapa Flow – 833 drown.
1815	Scots Greys lead charge at Waterloo.	1941	Clydebank bombed – 1200 killed.
1817	First issue of *The Scotsman* published.	1945	World War II ends. First SNP MP elected. Scottish Tourist Board formed.
1821	Population reaches 2 million.	1947	First Edinburgh International Festival held.
1822	George IV first monarch to visit Scotland in 171 years. Caledonian Canal opened.	1951	Population exceeds 5 million. IBM opens 'hi-tec' factory at Greenock.
1831	Scotland's first steam railway service runs between Glasgow and Garnkirk.	1952	First television transmission from Shotts, Lanarkshire.
1832	60,000 Scotsmen given vote. Cholera kills 40,000. Sir Walter Scott dies.	1955	Scotland's first nuclear power station, Chapel Cross, Dumfries-shire, opened.
1843	Disruption in Church of Scotland leads to formation of the Free Church.	1961	US nuclear submarine base opens in Holy Loch.
1853	First Scots settle in New Zealand. Andrew Usher invents 'blended whisky'.	1962	Last person hanged in Scotland, at Craiginches Gaol, Aberdeen.
1854	93rd Highlanders form 'thin red line' at battle of Balaclava, in Crimean War.	1964	Forth Road Bridge opened.
1867	Scottish Society of Women's Suffrage established in Edinburgh.	1967	Winnie Ewing wins Hamilton by-election for SNP. Celtic win European Cup.
1873	Scottish Football Association and Scottish Rugby Union founded.	1968	Church of Scotland admits women ministers.
1877	207 miners killed at Blantyre pit, Scotland's worst mining disaster.	1970	Commonwealth Games held in Edinburgh – the 'Friendly Games'.
1879	James Clerk Maxwell, physicist, dies. Tay Railway Bridge collapses, killing 79.	1974	Sullom Voe oil terminal, Shetland, opens.
1883	Boys' Brigade formed in Glasgow by William Smith.	1979	First Devolution referendum fails.
1886	Glasgow Underground opens.	1988	Piper Alpha oil platform explosion kills 226. Pan-Am plane blown up over Lockerbie – 270 killed.
1888	Keir Hardie forms Scottish Labour Party. 'Highers' introduced into schools.	1989	Introduction of Poll Tax leads to angry protests.
1889	Charles Rennie Mackintosh designs Glasgow Art School.	1995	Skye Bridge opens.
1890	Forth Rail Bridge opened.	1996	Stone of Destiny returns to Scotland – officially!
1900	Population exceeds 4.5 million (over 1 million in Glasgow alone).	1999	Scottish Parliament sits for first time since 1707.
1910	Scotland's first cinema opens in Glasgow.	2001	University of the Highlands and Islands established.
		2004	HM The Queen opens Holyrood Parliament building.
		2007	Scottish National Party becomes party of minority government in Scotland.
		2009	Convicted Lockerbie bomber released from prison on compassionate grounds.

Hirta Township, St Kilda: *Far out in the Atlantic lies the remote archipelago of St Kilda.*
Humans scratched a living there for over 4,000 years, but finally gave up their long struggle and great
hardships in 1930, when the remaining 36 islanders left their village for a new life on the mainland.

First published in Great Britain in 2010 by
Colin Baxter Photography Ltd., Grantown-on-Spey, Moray PH26 3NA, Scotland
www.colinbaxter.co.uk

Text by Chris Tabraham © Colin Baxter Photography 2010

Photographs © 2010 by: Arbuthnot Museum, Peterhead. Licensor www.scran.ac.uk: page 36;
Colin Baxter: Front cover, pages 1, 2, 4, 5, 8, 9, 10, 11, 12, 13 (top), 14, 15, 16, 17, 19, 20, 22, 24, 25, 26, 29 (top),
31, 32, 38, 39, 42, 44, 45, 48, Back cover; By permission of the British Library: page 18; Crown Copyright. Palace of Westminster
Collection: page 27; Dumfries & Galloway Council. Licensor www.scran.ac.uk: page 40; Glasgow City Libraries, Information and
Learning. Licensor www.scran.ac.uk: page 37; Glasgow Museums. Licensor www.scran.ac.uk: pages 21, 33; Glasgow Museums,
Art Gallery & Museum, Kelvingrove: page 6; National Museums of Scotland: page 13; National Museums of Scotland. Licensor
www.scran.co.uk: page 30 (top); Newsquest (Herald & Times). Licensor www.scran.ac.uk: page 43; The Royal Collection @
Her Majesty the Queen Elizabeth II: page 28; The Scotsman Publications Ltd: page 35 (bottom); Scottish Media Group: page 41;
Scottish National Portrait Gallery: pages 7, 23, 29, 30 (bottom); Springburn Museum Trust. Licensor www.scran.ac.uk: page 34;
University of Dundee, Department of Archives and Maunscripts. Licensor www.scran.ac.uk: page 35 (top).

ISBN 978-1-84107-409-2   Printed in China

Front Cover: Calanais, Lewis, Western Isles (top); Caerlaverock Castle, Dumfies & Galloway (bottom).
Back Cover: The Forth Bridge.   Page 1: Stone-Age village of Skara Brae, Orkney.